"If you want to know how to fight life's battles with hope, compassion and wisdom, read this book! Tim knows better than most what it takes to win on and off the field!"

—Jon Acuff, *New York Times* best-selling author

"From the first time you meet Tim Shaw, you know you'll never forget him. It may be his strength of character that impresses you, his sincerity or humility; but whatever it is, he is an inspiration to everyone he meets. He was before and is now—even carrying the extra burden of ALS. His message of hope and becoming all who God created you to be through whatever you face, which he expresses in this book, will lift you to live the life and have the impact in the world you were created to have."

—Mike Mularkey, former Head Coach,
Tennessee Titans

"When I first heard Tim had a book coming out, I got excited. Having played alongside him with the Titans, I got a chance to see Tim's passion, dedication, and will to fight to the end. He's a guy with a belief that he can conquer anything and has the faith to actually do it! What's even more admirable is how he continues to carry these qualities throughout his life, despite his current opponent being much tougher than those he faced on the football field. In *Blitz Your Life*, Tim says "I hate to admit it, but if anyone had ever been prepared to face a terminal illness such as ALS, it was probably me." Comments like that further prove the type of person and fighter Tim Shaw is and why I'm so proud to call him a friend."

—Jason McCourty, Cornerback,
New England Patriots

ON TURF AS IT IS IN HEAVEN

A 40-DAY DEVOTIONAL FOR ATHLETES

TIM SHAW

FOREWORD BY **DABO SWINNEY**

TWO-TIME NCAA NATIONAL CHAMPIONSHIP HEAD COACH

DEXTERITY

NASHVILLE

Dexterity, LLC
604 Magnolia LaneNashville, TN 37211
Copyright © 2019

Scripture quotations marked (NLT) or (TLB) are taken from the Holy Bible, New Living Translation, copyright ©1996, 2004, 2015 by Tyndale House Foundation or The Living Bible copyright © 1971. Used by permission of Tyndale House Publishers, Inc., Carol Stream, Illinois 60188. All rights reserved.

Scripture quotations marked (ESV) are from The ESV® Bible (The Holy Bible, English Standard Version®), copyright © 2001 by Crossway, a publishing ministry of Good News Publishers. Used by permission. All rights reserved.

Scripture quotations marked (NIV) or (NIrV) are taken from the Holy Bible, New International Version`, NIV`. Copyright © 1973, 1978, 1984, 2011 or the Holy Bible, New International Reader's Version`, NIrV` Copyright © 1995, 1996, 1998, 2014 by Biblica, Inc.™ Used by permission of Zondervan. All rights reserved worldwide. www.zondervan.com The "NIV," "New International Version," "NIrV," and "New International Reader's Version" are trademarks registered in the United States Patent and Trademark Office by Biblica, Inc.™

Scripture quotations marked (AMP) are taken from the Amplified Bible, Copyright © 1954, 1958, 1962, 1964, 1965, 1987 by The Lockman Foundation. Used by permission.

Scripture taken from the New King James Version`. Copyright © 1982 by Thomas Nelson. Used by permission.

First edition:
201910 9 8 7 6 5 4 3 2 1
Printed in the United States of America.

ISBN: 978-1-947297-14-2 (trade paper)
ISBN: 978-1-947297-15-9 (ebook)

Cover design by Gore Studios Inc. Interior design by Sarah Siegand. Writing and editorial contributions by Richard Sowienski.

The author gratefully acknowledges the photography of Donn Jones and Tennessee Football, Inc. for many of the photographs/still shots in this work. All rights reserved to Donn Jones/Tennessee Football, Inc. d/b/a Tennessee Titans for any such photographs. Further or additional use requires permission of the copyright holder: Tennessee Football, Inc. All works of Donn Jones under hire by Tennessee Football, Inc. are works made for hire and are the exclusive property of Tennessee Football, Inc. All rights reserved.

To the men who cared more about my future

as a man than my future as an athlete.

"When the game is over,

all that matters is knowing Christ."

—Tim Shaw

CONTENTS

We are all given a voice, though not necessarily audibly, that God wants heard. And we who are in this wonderful arena of sports have been given a unique platform to be heard from.

The incredible thing about Tim Shaw is that he has chosen to use his platform in a dynamic way, despite a condition no one would ever choose. He's a wonderful man of God, and I have had the privilege of meeting and greeting my fellow brother after hearing him speak of his faith several times. I admire his boldness to help make people aware of God while fighting for his life every day due to ALS. What's amazing to me is how he honors the Lord and speaks of God's goodness while battling this unkind disease. He is truly a living testament to the fact that we are not only called to trust our Lord, but also to honor His name no matter what our circumstances are. We all know that this can be much easier said than done. However, by God's grace, Tim has lived out this faith.

Tim was a great athlete, team player, and leader in his football career, which is one of the reasons his teammates voted for him as special teams captain while he played with the Tennessee Titans. With some of the same principles he used to attack and conquer the game of football all the way to the NFL, he now brings that same fervor to pursuing his walk with the Lord. This daily devotional will challenge you—you can feel Tim's passion and see his perspective with every word. His athletic illustrations are so practical and relevant to anyone seeking a deeper relationship with God, and I'm confident that God's wisdom through Tim's words will be a blessing to all.

Dabo Swinney
Head Football Coach,
Clemson University Tigers

As I write this, the NFL Draft is taking place right here in my hometown of Nashville, the place where I finished my own NFL career and where I had the honor of being named a Titan for Life. As I watched players' names be called and listened to follow-up interviews backstage, I was struck by the number of athletes and parents who thanked God for this great honor and blessing. Some quoted scripture, "With God all things are possible."

I can't help but think of the role faith played in my life as I pursued athletics, and how that faith in Jesus Christ guided and strengthened me. As an athlete, you know the sacrifices you've made—no matter what sport or what level. Being an athlete is difficult. In fact, the better an athlete you want to be, the more work is required and the harder it is. If it was easy, then everybody would do it! There is a price to pay just to be an athlete, let alone to be great. You have to deal with physical and mental stress. You face pressure to perform from inside yourself as well as from external forces. We athletes wrestle with failure at every turn. We pay a toll in countless hours spent in training. Of course, it's not all struggle and suffering. If all we got for our trouble was a varsity letter, we'd choose something else to do. We submit ourselves to the hardships in order to receive the benefits of being an athlete. We want a shot at the thrill that accompanies winning. We crave the satisfaction of accomplishment that comes from teamwork and improvement. And at the end of the day, we get to play and have fun! After all the ups and downs, it's all worth it when we're victorious.

Winning is great, but without God all our efforts would be in vain. 1 Timothy 4:8 says, "Physical training is good, but training for godliness is much better, promising benefits in this life and in the life to come." All the effort we give in hopes of excelling at sports will pale in comparison with the importance of time and effort put into our relationship with God. True, we learn so much from sports. Practical life skills like time management and teamwork, as well as internal values such as self-esteem and determination. Sure, training for sports is good, but like the verse says, training for godliness is so much better. When we train for godliness, we learn how to love ourselves and others, and—most important—we learn how to live a life with purpose and meaning that extends beyond our years as athletes.

I'd like to guarantee you that putting effort towards spiritual training will bring more victories in our sports, but it doesn't exactly work like that. I actually do believe that focusing on God will have a positive impact on athletic performance. I have no scientific evidence to support my theory, only my personal experience as an athlete for twenty-plus years. But I can guarantee that the benefits from time and effort with God far outweigh and outlast any athletic benefit.

We have been blessed with the ability to be athletes, and I believe we are meant to make the most of those God-given abilities. These daily devotionals are designed to enhance your spiritual training and as a byproduct, your athletic endeavors. Sometimes all we need is a push in the right direction or a spark to light the fire. I pray you feel that push or find that spark in your life with God. Yes, I hope this helps take your game to the next level, but even more so, I pray that it propels your life to new heights! I have wrestled with God at all levels of athletics, from Pee Wee leagues to the Big Ten to the NFL. My hope for you is that you pursue your relationship with God as if you are trying to win the championship of the world. There's no greater victory than victory in Jesus.

To provide that little extra push, each day I've included a whiteboard challenge for you. It's a method I've used through the years. Even now, I have a whiteboard hanging in my bathroom where I see it each morning. On it, I have my goals written. This board has been a constant reminder of where I want my focus. I change the contents of the board as my goals shift or are achieved. I encourage you to find something similar to my whiteboard to help keep your eyes on the prize. And accept my daily challenge to push yourself closer to whom God wants you to be.

Tim Shaw

WEEK ONE:

FUNDAMENTALS

WEEK 1
DAY ONE

ONE WAY

Jesus told him, "I am the way, the truth,
and the life. No one can come to the Father
except through me."

—John 14:6 NLT

"It's my way or the highway!"

Every athlete has gotten this message from a coach at one time or another. Either do things their way or don't play.

I never liked an ultimatum. Maybe it's just my aversion to authority, but why do coaches have to put it like that? Isn't there another way to say it? Does Coach even care about me and what's best for me?

It's a pretty clear choice for most of us. We want to play so we do what we're told, begrudgingly or not, even if we have a better way of doing things than our coach (and most of us think we do).

I've seen some athletes choose the other side of the ultimatum; they walked away. Right off the court, right out of practice. Sometimes our ego puffs up. Sometimes we're justified. We might refuse to believe that Coach wants the best for us, or we might just resent being given an ultimatum. At the end of the day, we have a choice. Some leave and never play again, some humble themselves and return. We can kick, squirm, argue or fight, but at the end of the day, what Coach says goes.

Jesus presents us with a choice as well. He is very clear that He is the one and only way to be with God the Father. The alternative is said to be a very hot and uncomfortable eternity. We are free to choose to be with Him or not. We may not be sure of our coaches' motives, but God's motives are clear. Love. Jesus's offer is full of love, and all we need to do is receive it. This choice is not one to be made begrudgingly. He is offering life when the alternative is death. At the risk of insulting God's offer, it's like being offered either a hot fudge brownie sundae or a tofu biscuit. Is there really a choice?

God sent his son to save us from eternal death and offer us forever spent with God. You might be thinking

"Why do I need saving?" Well the Bible tells us that we all have sin inside of us, and sin separates us from God. So Jesus is the bridge connecting us with God forever. Not only that, but as a follower of Jesus, we have the assurance of His promises for our lives today. For example, He will never leave us under even the worst circumstances; He loves and actually wants the best for us! We don't have to earn His love, and His great love will shine through us to others. We sometimes still think we have a better way, but in the end, there is no other way. But like with our coach, we do have a choice. We aren't puppets. We have free will. Let's accept God's gift of life and choose to play in this world and eternity with God.

WHITE BOARD CHALLENGE

Think about your relationship with Jesus. Is it time to go deeper, to make a commitment? What does that even mean? If you know that you need something more, the time is now. Find someone who knows God and ask them to show you. Find a Bible-preaching church or a

stranger preaching in the park. But giving your life to
God is the best thing you'll ever do. You can even go to
this website!

CHECK IT OUT:
**ransomedheart.com/prayer/ prayer-receive-
jesus-christ-savior**

WEEK 1
DAY TWO

PRAY LIKE IT'S OVERTIME

Rejoice always, pray without ceasing, give thanks
in all circumstances; for this is the will of God
in Christ Jesus for you.

—1 Thessalonians 5:16-18 ESV

I don't know if there's ever been more prayer at a football game then during the final moments in the third overtime of the 2006 Orange Bowl. My team, Penn State, was about to attempt a field goal that would beat Florida State and place us third in the whole country to end the year. People were praying hard, not because it was a difficult kick, but because our sophomore kicker had missed several that night, including one in each of the first two overtimes.

We were still alive because their kicker was equally unreliable.

Fans on both sides had hands clasped and heads bowed, begging and pleading with God for victory.

Players and coaches knelt and held hands on both sidelines.

I love this picture. A desperation for God. If only we could have this overtime desperation each day. If only we realized that without God, defeat is inevitable.

It seems like "pray without ceasing" is hyperbole, but it's not. God desires a constant communication with his people. He wants us to think of Him minute by minute and include Him in everything we do. Basically, it's admitting that He's the beginning and end, so we need Him in all things.

Life happens fast, and we all have non-stop schedules. I admit, I've always struggled with prayer. Keeping it real with you, I never thought I was praying enough or focused enough when I did pray. But I've improved my prayer life lately. What I really mean is that I've gotten more comfortable praying. My church hired a new pastor, and he brought with him the practice of prayer. Every Tuesday for an hour, in the middle of the day, we get together and pray. Everyone is welcome. I have learned so much and grown so much from this prayer time. Something Pastor Kevin said to us one day has stuck with me. "You will never regret one moment you spend in prayer."

For me, there are two types of conversations to have with God. One is a specifically dedicated time that I spend. I find a quiet place and tell God how I feel, what I desire, and what I'm going through. The other is the small chatter throughout my day. "God help me." "Thanks for that God." Even during a game, "Lord, give me calm, clear decision making." "God, I know you're with me." It's not constant, but it's my attempt to include and acknowledge God in every part of my day. "Oh, God, don't let their kicker make this kick!" By the way, don't worry: the Penn State kicker made the third overtime field goal, and the "good guys" won. I'm not saying that our side's prayers were more effective than the other, but I'm sure they didn't hurt.

WHITE BOARD CHALLENGE

Pray five different times today. It can be for a quick second or a lengthy session, but see what it's like to talk with God multiple times a day.

WEEK 1
DAY THREE

THE PLAYBOOK

Keep this Book of the Law always on your lips;
meditate on it day and night, so that you may be
careful to do everything written in it. Then you will be
prosperous and successful.

—Joshua 1:8 NIV

When I arrived as a rookie to play for the Carolina Panthers, one of the first things I received was the playbook. A four-inch thick, heavy three-ring binder. This thing had everything imaginable inside. Team rules, defensive plays, special teams plays, personnel phone numbers, drawings, policies, and probably even the Declaration of Independence! Everything.

It was overwhelming. None of it made sense at first. I wanted to make the team and play well, so I studied endlessly. Seemingly every free moment I wasn't eating or sleeping, I had my head in that massive binder.

Slowly but surely, I started to learn and understand.

God has given us the Bible as a playbook. It's huge and overwhelming and jam-packed with anything we can think of. The Bible is God's best way to communicate with us. It's full of stories and insights for us to learn from and seemingly endless knowledge and wisdom. We don't have to worry about making the team, but if we want to play well then we need to know the playbook. Slowly but surely, God will draw us to Him as we get to know Him through His Word.

After a few years, I became a Panthers veteran, and I knew the playbook pretty well, but I never stopped studying. There was always more to learn, and as I grew and changed, so did what I needed to know. God's Word works much the same way. The more we know, it seems the more there is to learn. A lifetime of plays taught by the Ultimate Coach.

I'm thankful that you've chosen to read these daily devotionals written by a washed-up linebacker who never went to seminary school—and if nothing else, I hope this sticks: make the Bible your most used resource for the rest of your life.

WHITE BOARD CHALLENGE

Get a Bible and start reading! Just because it's called the "Holy Bible" doesn't mean you can't get it a little dirty. Don't just read it, USE it! As you read, underline passages that are meaningful to you. Circle words or ideas that repeat. This often provides a strong clue of what may be important. Connect ideas with arrows. Write your observations, insights, and questions in the margin. Go ahead and mark it up! Think of this book as God's personal letter to you. A lifetime of wisdom for you to devour. It's like being in English class, except you're awake. (Just kidding, every English teacher I've ever had!)

Don't know where to start? Go with the book of Mark. Read a chapter each day until you finish the book. Then keep going!

WEEK 1
DAY FOUR

GET YOUR WORSHIP ON

Shout for joy to the LORD, all the earth. Worship
the LORD with gladness; come before him with
joyful songs. Know that the LORD is God. It is he
who made us, and we are his; we are his people,
the sheep of his pasture. Enter his gates with
thanksgiving and his courts with praise; give thanks
to him and praise his name.

—Psalm 100: 1-4 NIV

When I was a boy, I remember idolizing Michael
Jordan and Barry Sanders. I thought they were
the greatest athletes in the world. In my eyes,
they could do no wrong and should never lose.
I wouldn't say that I worshipped them, but they
ranked somewhere below Jesus and above the Pope.

We do that, don't we? We tend to put athletes
up on pedestals. In today's world, we do the same
with musicians, movie stars, and social media

darlings. We lift them up and admire them. Often, we can take this admiration too far, and it becomes unhealthy.

God alone is worthy of our praise. He is our creator and the creator of the universe. We can't begin to fathom the greatness of His love for us. He is all-knowing, all-powerful, and present everywhere at once.

God doesn't need our worship, but when we actually try to comprehend the God who made us, worship and admiration are a natural response. Over and over again, the Bible declares the glory of God and implores His people to praise His holy name.

Our culture exalts people and lifts them up, and while we wouldn't label it as worship, that's what it is. But as believers in Christ, we are called to worship God and God only.

I see worship as one of the three main important practices of someone in daily relationship with God, along with prayer and studying God's Word. I believe worship is a vital piece of the relationship.

I'll leave you to figure out what worship looks like for you. A lot of people assume worship means singing. But that is just one of the many ways to express reverence. I will tell you that worship involves humility and probably crosses into thanksgiving as well.

As athletes, we tend to be the ones seeking praise, but let's get into the habit of giving praise to the only one worthy of it: God above.

WHITE BOARD CHALLENGE

Today's challenge has two parts. First, name two things (or people) you hold in higher regard than you should. Put them in their proper place. Now secondly, spend time worshipping God. That's right, get your worship on!

WEEK 1
DAY FIVE

NO MATTER WHAT

Shadrach, Meshach, and Abednego replied to him, "King Nebuchadnezzar, we do not need to defend ourselves before you in this matter. If we are thrown into the blazing furnace, the God we serve is able to deliver us from it, and he will deliver us from Your Majesty's hand. **But even if he does not,** we want you to know, Your Majesty, that we will not serve your gods or worship the image of gold you have set up."

—Daniel 3:16 NIV, emphasis added

Sports will test you and so will life. The way I see it, you better have something firm to believe in and hold on to when it's testing time. For some athletes, that testing comes during a sports injury. I don't have a big injury story from my playing days, but I've always admired the athletes who suffered major injuries and fought back to return to their sports. It takes a lot of grit and willpower to come back after a tough injury. But what about the career ending injuries? What about the players who never make it back to the court or field?

Five years ago I was given a tough diagnosis. I can't tell you how many times I've asked God to take ALS from me, or how many well meaning people have prayed healing over my body. I sometimes think, "Man, what an amazing testimony that would be if I was healed. I would point all praise to God, and so many people would be impacted by the story." Yet here I am, still fighting this merciless disease. So why hasn't God solved my problem?

The Scripture for today tells an amazing story of three men who believe in God so strongly that they are willing to die rather than worship another God. The king promises to throw them into a blazing furnace if they don't bow to his statue. Their response shows what I aspire my faith to be. "Our God will save us. But even if he doesn't, that's okay" (a Tim Shaw paraphrase).

We ask God for a lot. In our toughest tests we beg for God to intervene. Does our faith and belief depend on God's response? It didn't to the three men standing between the king and the fire. I don't want it to for me. It's easy to praise God when we win. It's obvious to thank God after we return from an injury. But what about when we don't get what we want? When the opponent outstretches us at the finish line to win first place. When even after three surgeries, the knee just won't run like before. When my body continues to decline with no cure in sight.

I think this is the true test of our faith. Just as in our sport, we have to ask ourselves this: Who are we when we're losing? Do we shut down and give up, or do we fight for what we believe in? How do we respond to adversity? The Bible says that the testing of our faith develops perseverance. Well baby, I'm on perseverance human growth hormone, because my faith is undergoing test after test!

It's up to you to decide where you build your firm foundation, but I promise the tests will come. As for me, my entire life has proven to me that even when God doesn't seem to answer my cries for help, He will give me exactly what I need. This is a test in which I am determined to be as faithful as the men facing the fiery furnace and to praise God in victory or seeming defeat.

WHITE BOARD CHALLENGE

Read the entire fiery furnace story in Daniel Chapter
3. Check yourself to see if your belief is conditional,
dependent upon God doing something. If it is, this is
an area that you need to deal with.

WEEK TWO:
PRACTICE

WEEK 2
DAY ONE

Do not be deceived: God is not mocked,
for whatever one sows, that will he also reap.

—Galatians 6:7 ESV

There are a large number of laws that come from nature that throughout my life I have tried to defy. Gravity, friction, and good girls going for bad guys, just to name a few. But my all-time favorite law of nature is that we reap what we sow.

As an athlete, I owned this law; I built my reputation on it. I tried to enforce this law on everyone else too. You are what you eat. What you put in directly correlates to what you get out. I knew I was talented, but as a high school sophomore, I made a promise to myself that I would never be outworked throughout my football life. Now I can't sit here and tell you that nobody ever outworked me, but I can promise you that

I tried my best not to let that happen.

In sports as in life, it often feels like there isn't much we can control. I think that's why I clung to this law so tightly. It felt like something I had control over.

God tells us that we will reap what we sow. He doesn't say there will be immediate or visible justice or that all will appear right in the world, just that we will reap what we sow. It's nice to know that it isn't my job to police justice in the world. Life isn't fair. I'll leave the judging to God. I don't have time for it anyway.

Another cool part of this passage is the part about God not being mocked. It's saying, hey, you can fool people, you can lie to yourself, but you can't get one past God. He knows all and sees all. Actually, if He knows all, He doesn't need to see all. That is just a bonus. So don't bother trying to fool God, He already knows you took a shortcut when the coach wasn't looking. You may get away with shortcuts for a time, but eventually they will show up again.

It works the other way, too. That extra film study you put in that nobody seems to notice, God sees. It will benefit you one way or another someday.

The beauty of the law is that it also applies to all in a moral and spiritual sense. Verses eight and nine of Galatians 6 go on to say that if we give in to our own corrupt desires, planting seeds of evil, we will reap spiritual decay. But if we plant good things of the Spirit, we'll reap eternal life. The Amplified Bible puts it this way: "Let us not grow weary or become discouraged in doing good, for at the proper time we will reap, if we do not give in."

I believe that there is always more going on than I know or can see. God knows what's best for me, even when I don't like it or think it's right. We may never know why things are the way they are, so I choose to focus on what I can control. I just keep sowing and believing God will make good on his promise.

WHITE BOARD CHALLENGE

Do one thing today that you know will benefit you in the future. Not something you had already planned on doing. Something else: more repetitions, extra laps, more time with your least favorite subject, more prayer.

Bonus: keep at it tomorrow and the next day. Maybe it will become a habit.

NO REPEAT OFFENDERS

You were taught, with regard to your former way of life,
to put off your old self, which is being corrupted by its
deceitful desires; to be made new in the attitude of
your minds; and to put on the new self, created to be
like God in true righteousness and holiness.

—Ephesians 4:22-24 NIV

It's almost never pleasant getting correction from
a coach. I think most sports are like football in
the way that you better develop some thick skin,
or you'll be walking around with hurt feelings all
the time. I remember my first minicamp with the
Panthers after being drafted. Coach corrected me
during a linebacker drill, and then a player that
went after me made the same mistake I had made.
Coach wasn't happy and took the opportunity to
tell the group that he doesn't mind coaching us, but
there's nothing he likes less than a repeat offender.

Not just the same guy repeating a mistake, but somebody else making the same mistake that was just corrected. The repeat offender was worse than the original because now we should know better. You bet I took that with me through my NFL career and into life.

Am I the only one who finds it ironic that we hate to repeat mistakes in our sports lives but will blatantly choose to keep going back to the same no-good activities in our everyday lives? Just me? Okay, amen, lights and walls. (I had a chaplain who would say that when nobody responded to a good point.)

I'll admit, I was a repeat offender when it came to some of my personal habits. I knew the right thing to do. I had been corrected, but I just kept choosing to make the same mistakes over and over.

I won't tell you that God sees repeat offenders as worse than the originals. The Bible is clear, sin is sin, and all of it separates us from God. But I can tell you this, avoiding mistakes saves us from what can be harmful consequences and repercussions.

God gives us his Word, and He gives us the example of others to save us from some of those heartaches and scars.

I'm thankful that no matter how many times I make the same dumb mistakes, God forgives me and loves me, but I'm going to try to take my spiritual life as seriously as my sport and cut out the repeats.

WHITE BOARD CHALLENGE

Time for an honest conversation with yourself. Are there areas that you are willingly repeating mistakes? First, admit it. Then ask God for the desire to change and the strength to do so.

WEEK 2
DAY THREE

HATERS GONNA HATE

Don't answer the foolish arguments of fools,
or you will become as foolish as they are.

—Proverbs 26:4 NLT

I'm sure someone out there has had the foresight to translate the Bible into a "Street Edition." If they haven't, there's your big idea—you're welcome. In the street translation of Proverbs 26:4, it reads, "Haters gonna hate. Let 'em."

The school district I grew up in was a small public school district just outside of Detroit, Michigan. So that's where my brothers and I went.

Clarenceville was good to our family. As my success in football grew larger and stretched further, there was one sentiment attached to my name seemingly more often than the rest. "*I was just a big fish in a small pond.*" First of all, they weren't wrong. I was big. And C'ville was small. I just prefer to be likened to something tougher than a fish. How about a big bear in a small campground or a big rhino in a small game reserve? (Are rhinos herbivores? Whoops.) So as I piled up the state record in touchdowns scored and rushing yards, they said that I was doing it against poor competition. So maybe I was, and maybe I wasn't. The point is that there is always going to be noise and nonsense happening around us, but we need to focus on what God has called us to do and ignore everything else. People will say all types of crazy stuff that is irrelevant just to hear their own voices. The challenge is blocking out the garbage and listening to the voice of God. I'm sure that when I went on to start for three years at the huge Penn State pond, those same big-fish people found someone else to hate on.

My high school haters are one example of what the Bible calls fools. They are everywhere. (And if you can't find one, then it's probably you! Just kidding.) I think a fool is either someone who knows the right thing to do yet does the opposite, or doesn't know the right thing at all but claims they do. A fool is someone trying to distract you from what God has for you. They come in all shapes and sizes. And beware of the ones that look cute and talk smooth. Much like a lot of the things in life, the more we seek God, the more we can identify the fools in our lives. Now don't go calling your coach a fool next time they yank you from a game. Ask God for discernment when you come across something or someone that is testing your character. It might be a heckler in the stands, a reporter, or even a teammate.

I've found it to be one of the most difficult things ever to do: to *not* correct someone when you know they are wrong. It's super tough but very rewarding when achieved. I think it's called taking the high road. Especially with a fool, you're better off letting them be. In my case, I just went back to fishing in my tiny pool. Or something like that.

WHITE BOARD CHALLENGE

Identify the "fools" in your life, the voices you need to ignore. Offer their names up to God and release yourself from any power their words have. Now brush your shoulders off and keep it movin'!

WHAT YOU LOOKIN' AT, WILLIS?

The eye is the lamp of the body. If your eyes are
healthy, your whole body will be full of light.
But if your eyes are unhealthy, your whole body
will be full of darkness. If then the light within you
is darkness, how great is that darkness!

—Matthew 6:22-23 NIV

"You have bad eyes!" I can still hear my linebacker
coach yelling. "Keep your eyes on your luggage!"

In football, like most sports, there are key
fundamentals that make a huge difference. It might
seem like the most basic element, but without the
basics even the most highly trained player can look
like a novice. Every sport has them. Footwork, hand
position, leverage, and many more. In football, one
of those key fundamentals is eye discipline.

There's so much to see during a football play,
so much going on, that if you aren't focused on

the correct thing, you will be lost. You must train your eyes to see your assignment, or you'll surely be fooled. That's why my coach was yelling at me. I got caught looking at the ball when I should have been watching my man!

This is a vital life application. So critical for health, both spiritual and otherwise. If your eyes are healthy, your whole body will be healthy. What you put in front of your eyes, somehow makes its way to your brain and your heart. I don't know how, it's just science. So when I was staring at girls all day long, I magically thought about girls when I was supposed to be thinking about school or football. No one can probably relate to that one (wink wink). This goes hand in hand with the "reap what you sow" and "you are what you eat" doctrines.

On the flip side, when we focus our view in the right direction, we head that way. You ever notice when you're walking or driving, if you turn your vision to the right or left, you tend to drift that way? It's true. Our eyes steer the ship. So we must do our best to keep our eyes fixed on things that would make our mothers proud. Oh, and God in heaven.

WHITE BOARD CHALLENGE

Take five minutes today to visualize where you want to go. Both athletically and in life. Then take a minute to picture the things that could or already do distract you from where you want to go. Now pray and ask God to help keep your eyes fixed on the right things. You're on your way!

MORE PREP, LESS HAIL MARY

"Physical training is good, but training for
godliness is much better, promising benefits in this
life and in the life to come."

—1 Timothy 4:8 NLT

Every athlete remembers the wins and losses, but we
all know that it was the grueling hours of training we
endured that made the victory so sweet and the losses so
rough. I swear I remember the preparation more clearly
than some of the games. Maybe because like a lot of
sports, in football you train a great deal more than you
play. You train for hours and hours and months and
months, only to play ten games in high school, thirteen
in college, sixteen in the pros.

The training is where you make your money,
where you hone your craft. Practice is where you build
chemistry and communication with your teammates.
All this comes together on game day to hopefully

produce a winning effort. The fans don't see the hours of sacrifice. They just show up on game day and expect you to perform. But without all the hard work, game day is a mess.

This is much like our spiritual walk with God. Many of us wait to call on God until we are in a tough spot. Somebody is ill, money is short, or we're lost. But God wants to be like your set of dumbbells in the weight room rather than your Hail Mary pass at the end of the game. (Stay with me here.) He wants us to spend time with Him daily, do all types of exercises with Him, let Him help us get stronger, pick Him up, throw Him down, scream and grunt and sweat. If we do exercise regularly with dumbbells like prayer and church and God's Word, then we'll be ready for game day or when tragedy strikes. God actually doesn't mind last-minute heroics. He's quite good at them. But He'd prefer that we train for battle with Him, so we can fight alongside rather than only calling on Him when we need him. He isn't a genie after all. This doesn't mean we shouldn't call on Him when we need Him; we should. Or that He only answers us if we've been "working out" with Him daily. Or that if we have been spending time training with God, we will get what we want.

Deep breath.

All of this to say, God wants a personal relationship with us. An everyday, good, bad, ugly, real relationship. When game day comes, in the form of tragedy or opportunity, you will be ready to go through it with God. Like all the training for your sport, people don't need to see or know about all the spiritual training you're doing, but when game day comes it will be obvious that God is with you.

WHITE BOARD CHALLENGE

What's your daily spiritual workout plan? We need one. So figure it out, write it down, and get to training. While you're at it, put your plan where you will see it daily.

WEEK THREE:

TEAM

› TEAMWORK MAKES THE DREAM WORK ‹

There is one body, but it has many parts. Even though it
has many parts, they make up one body. It is the same
with Christ. We were all baptized by one Holy Spirit
into one body. It didn't matter whether we were Jews
or Gentiles, slaves or free people. We were all given the
same Spirit to drink. The body is not made up of just
one part. It has many parts. Suppose the foot says,
"I am not a hand. So I don't belong to the body." It is
still part of the body. And suppose the ear says,
"I am not an eye. So I don't belong to the body." It is
still part of the body. If the whole body were an eye,
how could it hear? If the whole body were an ear,
how could it smell?

—1 Corinthians 12:12-17 NIRV

Teamwork. It's probably one of the first concepts every
young athlete is taught. No matter the sport, so long
as there's more than one player per side, teamwork is
critical. The team that works best together gives itself
the best chance to win.

Every teammate has a job to do and the good teams rely on each other. I played linebacker so my job was to cover and tackle. Call on me to kick the game winning field goal or throw a touchdown pass and you bet your top dollar we will lose. That's not my job. We need a kicker and quarterback for that.

The Bible tells us that the Christian body is a team too. We all have different roles. Some have a gift to teach or to encourage, others have a gift of service or hospitality, while others have a gift of wisdom or knowledge, among others. We are to do our roles to our fullest potential and lean on others to fulfill their roles. If one wins, we all win. If one loses, we all lose. Sound familiar?

We aren't meant to be good at everything or to do it alone. Find some other believers and work together. This is where a family, a team, Bible study group, or church body come into play. At Penn State I went to the Athletes in Action Bible study. Once a week I got to intentionally be around people who wanted to follow God. That encouraged me to keep following. It showed me that there were lots of people who were different from me and had different talents than me who were on my team.

The coolest thing is that no part of the body or team is more important than the other. Sure the quarterback gets the TV commercial, but any true athlete knows that the quarterback is nothing without the offensive line to block for him and receivers to catch his passes. So the preacher may get the attention, but in God's army, the man or woman feeding the hungry is just as valuable.

Win together. Lose together. Team.

WHITE BOARD CHALLENGE

It's time to figure out what your spiritual gifts are. What part of the team are you? Find a spiritual gifts test and take it! There are a million online. Here's the one I just took.

CHECK IT OUT:

sdrock.com/giftstest/new

A TALE OF TWO JONS

"Do all that you have in mind," his armor-bearer said.
"Go ahead; I am with you heart and soul."

—1 Samuel 14:7 NIV

This has got to be one of the coolest stories told in the
Bible. Definitely one of my favorites. Take the time to
read the entire thing in 1 Samuel. Jonathan basically just
decides that he's going to scale a cliff and kill a bunch of
Philistines. Pretty much by himself—well with God, of
course. His servant, knowing exactly what Jonathan was
doing, simply says, "I got your back." So they go and
kill a bunch of Philistines together.

We all want that type of loyalty. Don't we? Maybe
the better question is, do we give this type of loyalty to
anyone else? One of the characteristics of a teammate is
to look out for each other, but would you follow your
teammates up a cliff and into a fight with your rival?

Do you have a best friend or family member you would do absolutely anything for? Loyalty like this is priceless.

God promises to never leave us or forget about us and models the ultimate loyalty for us.

Here's an example of loyalty from my playing days. I had roomed with Jon Beason before every game for a year and a half. We were drafted together by the Carolina Panthers, both linebackers, and good friends, so we shared a hotel room. After the last preseason game our second year, I was cut from the team. Just that easy, I was gone! Jon and I stayed in touch as the season progressed, and about three weeks in I asked, "Who did they stick in your room with you?" I was just curious.

"They tried to put someone in here, but I wouldn't let them take your bed."

"What! C'mon man. You don't have to do that."

"Naww, Timmy, it isn't right. I'm saving your bed for when they pick you back up."

Wow! Not only did he fight to keep my bed, but he also had to pay for it out of his own pocket. It was very uncommon a second year player be allowed to have his own room, but Jon fought for me. Might sound like no big deal, but it would have been much easier for Jon to just accept a new roommate, and nobody would have blamed him. That was the way it was. But Jon honored me by showing great loyalty.

I count myself blessed and fortunate to have someone do something like that for me. Yes, I had been a loyal friend to Jon, but I didn't deserve that. But that's what God does for us: sticks up for us when we don't deserve it, time and time again. And, with fear of taking the analogy too far, God always saves our spot for us. Regardless of anything else, God's loyalty will never expire.

Let's strive to be as loyal as Jonathan's sword bearer and my teammate Jon. But more than that, let's not forget God's loyalty for us.

WHITE BOARD CHALLENGE

Thank the person who has shown loyalty to you. And make a mental note of where your loyalty needs improvement.

WEEK 3
DAY THREE

A friend loves at all times, and a brother is
born for a time of adversity.

—Proverbs 17:17 NIV

One of the best things about sports is the relationships.
From peewee to pro, it's the relationships that outlast
the victories.

You hear across all sports that the best teams are
the closest knit. It makes sense. If you care about your
teammates, then you'll do whatever you can to not let
them down. You'll train hard, study more, and make
sure you're prepared to carry your weight. You'll stand
up for each other and protect each other. Doesn't matter
if you're at center court or in the mall after school,
teammates stick together.

I've been lucky enough to keep a solid friend or two
from each team I was on, and a few I met outside of sports

as well. I felt so much love from these guys, as well as my three biological brothers, that I tattooed their initials on my forearm. Whenever I'm in a tough spot, I look down and remember that there are a bunch of guys who have my back. And they have had my back—some on the gridiron and some in my hardest moments in life. We may not still be the closest of friends today, but I know that if I needed them, they would be there. And that's enough.

Do you have people who have your back? Finding those people and building those relationships have to be top priority. You don't have to look far. If they aren't on your team, then they're in your class or at your job. Maybe at your church or gym. They'll be the ones wearing the t-shirts that say "loyalty needed?" Don't forget it's a two-way street. Friendship and loyalty go both ways. Both are built through shared experience and testing moments. When the moments arise, step up and be there. Loyalty given is loyalty earned.

For all that we go through as athletes, brotherhood/ sisterhood is one of our rewards. If you're as lucky as me, you might even end up with a tattoo that reminds you how great of a reward it is.

WHITE BOARD CHALLENGE

Hang time. Make an intentional effort to spend quality time with a friend. Maybe an overdue hang, a friend going through a tough time, or a first-time hang with someone new. Give the time and the long-term rewards will come.

WEEK 3
DAY FOUR

FOOLISH TO SOME

For the message of the cross is foolishness
to those who are perishing, but to us who are
being saved it is the power of God.

—1 Corinthians 1:18 NIV

My dad once went with my brother Drew on a recruiting visit to the University of Toledo and sat in a meeting with the linebacker coach. Now you have to understand that my dad, even though he has four athletes for sons, doesn't know the third thing about football. Let's just say, after the ball is snapped, he doesn't know a draw from a screen or a blitz from a coverage. God bless him; we love him that way, and he loves us right back.

So Dad was sitting in this defensive meeting taking notes, as he tended to do, and was understanding every twenty-seventh word but unable to make sense of a complete sentence. The language being spoken between Drew and the coach was entirely English and entirely intelligible, yet to Dad it may as well have been ancient Egyptian. He comes home from the visit with his notebook and proudly reads the nonsensical phrases (to him) one after another, making a silly, if not comical display, of the language of football. "The Mike needs to run with the vertical. In Tampa, all zone eyes are reading the Q. We are a heavy zone dog with a sprinkle of man free. Shoot the hands! Hair trigger! Climb to contact and dip and rip!"

I wonder if we consider what others think when they hear us talking about our faith in God. Maybe to people who don't believe in God, we sound like we're talking a different language. Maybe we sound foolish. To us, it makes complete sense. But to others, it may sound like the linebacker coach sounded to my dad.

Sometimes it's okay to look foolish. God says that to those who don't know better or who have hard hearts, the things of God will be nonsense. It's not our responsibility to convince people that we're not crazy or that God is awesome, but only to love them. God is great at softening hearts and opening minds. We just need to show people love.

My encouragement to you today is to be yourself around your teammates. Don't be afraid to look or sound a little foolish because you're living for God. You don't have to preach to your team either, just be true to the Holy Spirit inside you. Your team will respect you for who you are, and I'll bet God will work some magic along the way.

WHITE BOARD CHALLENGE

I'm challenging you to do something "foolish" today! Ask someone, a teammate or classmate, what they think about God. And just have an honest conversation about it. Who knows what might come of such foolishness?

WEEK 3
DAY FIVE

My dear brothers and sisters, take note of this:
Everyone should be quick to listen, slow to speak and
slow to become angry,

—James 1:19 NIV

Well, well, well. If you're like me at all, then you've been caught with your foot in your mouth more times than you'd like to remember. Maybe my most epic display of toes on tongue was when I made fun of a girl in a picture who turned out to be my college roommate's sister. My six-foot seven offensive lineman roommate! Whoops! I hope you haven't had as embarrassing a moment as that, but it's safe to assume we've all had moments where our mouth has gotten us into trouble.

I don't know if it's biblical, but I like the saying, "God gave you two ears and one mouth for a reason." The majority of the time it's better to listen than to speak.

As athletes, communication is typically of paramount importance to our success, unless your sport is fencing or downhill skiing. Knowing when not to communicate can be just as important, if not more important, than when to communicate. Learning the art of listening is a valuable life skill. We need to be able to receive information and instruction, not only from our coaches, but from teachers, parents, and bosses too. Sure, being able to deliver a message is a valuable skill, but if you don't know how to listen, then nobody will want to hear what you have to say. Really, any relationship you have will benefit from the skill of listening.

Thankfully, and I say this with my eyes half rolled back, we have coaches to help us master the art of listening. I know I did. "You wanna talk? Run a suicide." "Didn't hear my instructions clearly? That is going to cost you some pushups." This tough love coaching helps athletes learn how to listen, painful as it may be.

Jesus models what it is to be a good listener. Even though the Bible records a lot of what Jesus said, we also see countless instances where He is the listener.

People were forever bringing their problems to Jesus, and He was quick to listen. He knew how to ask a good question too, and then show His love by listening to the response.

Like Jesus, good athletes know how to communicate. More importantly, they know how to listen.

WHITE BOARD CHALLENGE

Be intentional about listening today. See if you can catch yourself about to speak quickly or harshly and listen a little more. It will make a big difference.

WEEK FOUR:

ACCOUNTABILITY

MAKE EACH OTHER BETTER

As iron sharpens iron, so one person sharpens another.

—Proverbs 27:17 NIV

Most of my time in the NFL was spent on the scout team. This just means that while our offense was practicing to play against that week's opponent, I would play the role of mimicking that team's defense, running their plays and showing their tendencies. This could be a thankless task and a bit mindless, so to keep it interesting my teammates and I would compete. Who could tag the ball carrier, cause a fumble, or intercept a pass? We were competing but really that was our way of holding each other accountable for working hard. The prize? A mighty dollar. You wouldn't believe how hard we worked to win that dollar. Because it wasn't about the dollar but about not letting our teammates down. And really, if you zoom out for the big picture, it was about winning. If winning was the top of the ladder and the dollar was the bottom rung, in between was self-respect, desire to improve, fear of losing a job, and respect for teammates.

The point is that no matter what the motivation is, accountability can help. We wouldn't let our teammates slack off or settle for less than hard work. As athletes, we should have different accountability measures in place to help us achieve our goals.

Our spiritual lives are no different. Use the methods you learned from sports to keep you on track towards your spiritual growth. I find it absolutely necessary to have some people in my life who will ask me the tough questions. "Are you spending time with God daily?" "Hey, I know you had been struggling with such and such, how is that going?" "Have you been to those websites that get you off track?" Real stuff! I'm not talking about feel-good churchy stuff, but useful, helpful, real stuff that makes a difference in your life.

We all need people who care enough to ask and then speak truth to us. And we have to be honest enough to be real and hear what they say. Without care and honesty on both sides, it's wasted energy. I couldn't lie to my scout team partners. Everything we did was caught on film anyway. And it definitely wouldn't help us win. If the goal is to be the best version of ourselves that we can be, let's put accountability in place to help with that!

WHITE BOARD CHALLENGE

Do you have people who hold you accountable? If you don't, your challenge is to find at least one person who can do that for you and to ask them to fill that role. Do it today! If you have accountability already, your challenge is to identify one specific item or area of your life that needs fresh attention. Take that specific need to an accountability partner and ask their involvement.

MENTORLESS: WILL WORK FOR WISDOM

A wise man will hear and increase in learning, and a man of understanding will attain wise counsel.

—Proverbs 1:5 NKJV

I can look back on my journey as an athlete and identify at least one person at each step who took an intentional interest in my spiritual growth. In high school it was Pastor Keift. Tim McGill in college. Bunk, AJ, and Reggie in the pros. There is no doubt that without these men I would be a lot less mature in my Christian life. I'm so thankful for what these people taught me and more so the love they showed me.

I love how Jesus seemingly walks up to each disciple and says, "Hey, you. Yeah, you. Come with me." I believe God does that, but in my experience, mentors typically don't. For most of the mentors I've had throughout life, I've been the one to ask for some of their time.

It's almost like that's the buy in. They can't make it too easy or we wouldn't go for it. I knew Reggie Pleasant was the team chaplain for the Titans, but if I wanted more than a player's Bible study once a week and a quick pregame service, I was going to have to ask, "Hey, could we meet one on one some time?"

I knew that if I wanted to go deeper and learn more, then I needed to spend some intentional time with someone who knew a whole lot more than me. That became my formula for spiritual growth. No matter what team I was on—college, high school, or pro—I spent time with a wiser man on a regular basis, so I could navigate my sports life with the God who made me. Mr. Keift would meet with a couple guys and me on Saturday morning at Burger King for a little Jesus and a little hash browns. Tim and I met at the academic center before football meetings. I'd spend time with Bunk, AJ and Reggie around the team facility during the season and wherever else during the off-season. The point is that we made it a priority to spend the time. I have no doubt that those relationships shaped the trajectory of my life.

Sure we need mentors in athletics, too. Coaches oftentimes fill that role, but it can be good to have other mentors as well. And once again I want you to think bigger than your sport. I urge you to find someone who can mentor you on the spiritual side of things. The benefits will last a lifetime and beyond! I know they have for me.

WHITE BOARD CHALLENGE

Do you have a mentor? Find one! The criteria can be as simple as they appear wiser than you when it comes to spiritual things. Ask them if they will meet with you one on one. It's a big, bold step, but so vital and so worth it.

OUR DAILY BREAD

All Scripture is breathed out by God and profitable for teaching, for reproof, for correction, and for training in righteousness, that the man of God may be complete, equipped for every good work.

—2 Timothy 3:16-17 ESV

In my second year as a Titan, we signed veteran quarterback Matt Hasselbeck. He was a proven winner and impacted our locker room right away. More than that, Matt was a Christian with a genuine way of living.

Matt quickly introduced the team to the *Daily Bread* game. *Our Daily Bread* was a short devotional guys could read. Each entry was made up of a Bible verse paired with a quick story and application. The game went like this: once you agreed to play, every day when you were at the facility you were fair game. Anybody in the game could test to see if you had read your *Daily*

Bread. If done well, this was tactfully entered into conversation, referencing something from the *Bread*. If the tested player failed to have read it, he paid a dollar to the pot. And it wasn't just one and done either. As long as you were at the facility, you could be tested over and over, even if you already owed a dollar. At the end of the season, we donated all the money earned from the game.

The game got guys to get some daily scripture in and talk about it. Like most locker rooms, ours wasn't usually filled with the sounds of Bible study. The typical everyday conversations leaned more towards HBO street-style rather than PBS educational-style language. But with the *Bread* game, guys who weren't Christians or would never read the Bible or go to church were being exposed to the things of God, because they wanted in on the game. Man, we had fun with that game! Guys were so competitive that they didn't want to get caught not knowing their *Bread*. I heard that Matt even tried to catch guys in their cars on the way to work, but as far as I know that's illegal until you pull onto team property. Matt was always one to stretch the rules.

I'm forever grateful to Matt for his friendship and for showing me how to live out my faith and bring others along. Oh, and I'm still reading *Our Daily Bread*.

WHITE BOARD CHALLENGE

Find a daily devotional to read. Oh, wait. This is one! Bring someone along for the journey. Whether this devotional or another, share the daily impact of the Word with others. It's always better together.

DOUBLE YOUR TALENTS

"And he also who had the two talents came forward, saying, 'Master, you delivered to me two talents; here, I have made two talents more.' His master said to him, 'Well done, good and faithful servant. You have been faithful over a little; I will set you over much. Enter into the joy of your master.'"

—Matthew 25:22-23 ESV

We all know that person, probably more than one, who is ultra-gifted but can never seem to bring his or her game up to the level of their potential. You know the one: couldn't keep the grades up so became ineligible, is just plain lazy, or doesn't care enough to do more than the bare minimum. We've all had teammates like this over the years.

When I read the parable of the talents, I think about all the "wasted talent" I've seen over my time in sports, and I wonder what talent I've wasted.

(Fun fact: When Jesus told this parable, a talent meant a large amount of money. It's cool that we can substitute the word "gifts" for an up-to-date meaning.)

Truth is, God has given each and every one of us different amounts to use. Different amounts of what? Anything and everything. Height, brain capacity, wit, musical abilities, vision, pain threshold, foot speed. And on and on. As far as we know, it isn't fair. There's no rhyme or reason why I have an enormous head and you can spit a watermelon seed halfway across the backyard. Those are the hands we were dealt.

The great news is that all we have to do is make the most of what we've been given. Do the best with what you have. The goal is to reach your God-given potential. If God gave you Olympic speed, then you should nurture that gift, work and grow it, use it for God's glory. And see where that speed will take you. If you sit on it, take it for granted, minimize it, then at the end of your life you will hear, "You wicked and lazy servant." On the other hand, if you have the ability to be a good high school pitcher, then God doesn't expect you to make the major leagues.

But He is counting on you to use all you've got for your school.

Use all you have been given. There isn't much worse than an unused gift. That's why we remember the underachievers we've known and imagine what could have been. I think we forget that God gave us things for us specifically. Nobody else. Me! You! But too often we devalue the very thing that makes us special because it isn't what we want or it isn't popular. We are meant to embrace what we have and make the most of it! To push it to its limits and let the chips fall where they may.

It isn't complicated at the end of the day. I don't want to waste what I've been given. I want to hear, "Well done, good and faithful servant."

WHITE BOARD CHALLENGE

Are you making the most of the gifts you have? I challenge you to name one gift you have that is underutilized. It could be athletic or otherwise. Now that you've named it, decide on a way to better use it.

COPY THAT

Imitate God, therefore, in everything you do, because you are his dear children. Live a life filled with love, following the example of Christ. He loved us and offered himself as a sacrifice for us, a pleasing aroma to God.

—Ephesians 5:1-2 NLT

I sadly don't know who to credit for one of the best pieces of advice I've ever received. Whoever it was said this: "Find someone whom you want to be like, and follow them." This advice helped shape my athletic career and even my life.

As a high school freshman it was Walter Ragland, the senior all-state tailback who was the star of the team. I watched how hard he worked and tried to keep up with him. I paid careful attention to the humble way he carried himself and treated people. I did what I could to be like Walter.

Jesus Christ is the ultimate example for us to follow. There's no better person to imitate. We have God's Word to show us Christ's life, and He also puts people in our lives to serve as examples, too.

When I got to Penn State, veterans like Sean McHugh and Mike Lucac were a couple of the guys I tried to imitate. Everywhere I played, I found someone who could do something I wanted to do or knew something I wanted to know, and I'd follow them. Every pro team I made it to, after a quick assessment, I'd find someone to imitate. I'd usually pick the guy acting the craziest and having the most fun. Okay, maybe that's a bit of an exaggeration, but I did gravitate towards the ones who were a little off, like me! They didn't always have to be older, just worth copying. Sometimes I would copy from a distance and other times I'd imitate up close. I'm not talking about anything creepy here. Don't follow too closely. That's called stalking, and that is frowned upon in civilized countries. Keep it cool and friendly, and you'll be all right.

See, no matter what level you are at, there's always something more to learn.

I hope that by me following the example of some great guys, I not only became a better football player but a better person. And somewhere along the way, I became a man worth following. That's how it's supposed to work. Follow my example as I follow Christ.

No matter who we're following, let's not forget the ultimate model that God gave us.

Oh, and whoever gave me that advice all those years ago, thanks, I owe you one!

WHITE BOARD CHALLENGE

Find and follow. Evaluate your team, classmates, or anyone within eyesight. Choose a worthwhile example. Now follow! It's okay, imitation is the best form of flattery.

WEEK FIVE:
STRUGGLES

LIFE CAN SUCK

"I have told you these things, so that in me you may
have peace. In this world you will have trouble. But
take heart! I have overcome the world."

—John 16:33 NIV

Ask me what I'm most proud of regarding my athletic
career and I'll probably tell you I'm most proud of
my durability. I never missed a game due to injury all
through high school and never in the NFL either. I
technically didn't miss any in college either, because I
still suited up when I was hurt and wound up standing
on the sidelines all game.

My first year as a starter at Penn State, I sprained
an ankle a few games into the season. The pain was
bearable, but my movement was limited. Man, I hated
missing time. I mean time doing anything football
related. Practice, lifting, and it goes without saying,

the actual game! I felt like a castaway. Useless, lonely, frustrated. I had done so much and worked so hard to earn that time on the field. To watch it pass by because of a stupid injury was pure torture.

Thankfully, the ankle only kept me sidelined for a couple games, then it was back to fighting the other battles at hand.

Playing sports can be tough. Heck, life is tough. Every game, practice, and even workout has its challenges. We do our best to push through those moments and win. But for most of us, we lose more than we want to admit. Oftentimes, it's bigger than our sport. An injury cannot only keep us from performing but can affect us off the court too. An ill family member puts a dark cloud over every aspect of life. If we're struggling with a relationship, we might let that impact our game. This world is complicated and doesn't give us a pass just because we're athletes.

Life is tragic! There's no avoiding it. But take heart, for God has conquered life and death. God is faithful. That doesn't mean the problems disappear or the tough times become easy, but it does mean that for all who have a relationship with Christ, God has promised to be with you through the tough times and give you peace in the midst of problems.

Let's seek God in the face of our trials and allow His Holy Spirit to walk with us to the other side.

WHITE BOARD CHALLENGE

What do you need to give over to God today? Choose your toughest battle you're currently facing. Spend a few minutes or more asking God to bring peace to you and the situation.

STAY ON GUARD!

The sinful nature wants to do evil, which is just the opposite of what the Spirit wants. And the Spirit gives us desires that are the opposite of what the sinful nature desires. These two forces are constantly fighting each other, so you are not free to carry out your good intentions.

—Galatians 5:17 NLT

Whenever football was going on, I was one of the most disciplined athletes I knew. But the off-season was a different story. Many athletes seem to have the same issue. It's funny really, how we can be so committed and focused but then be unmotivated and irresponsible.

You've probably heard Proverbs 16:27 (TLB), and I'm here to tell you it's true, "Idle hands are the Devil's playground." Especially for athletes! If you take away our structure and give us a little freedom, shoot, all bets are off, there's no telling what we'll do. When did we always hear the "stay out of trouble" speeches? No, not during the season or in the heart of winter workouts. Yup, right before a break. The coaches knew it and so did we.

I always worried about a teammate or two getting into trouble during off time, but my issue was trading good habits in for some not-so-good ones. If I was in the habit of spending the first part of my day with God, when I got a break from ball, I might sleep in and skip that time with God all together. And if I skipped time with God, I found my mind concentrating on different stuff. Next thing I knew, I was off chasing girls at all hours of the night, because I had no football to wake up for the next day, and I hadn't set my mind on the right things per my usual routine. It was a slippery slope for me. Was? Is.

Don't kid yourself, the Devil is always on the move, just waiting for us to give him an opening. We all have a sinful nature even after we've given our lives to Christ. That sinful nature is in constant opposition to the Holy Spirit inside us. If we don't continue to feed the spirit, the sinful nature will work its way in and try to take over. Just like we train our minds and bodies for our sport, we also need to continue to train our minds and spirits to fight against sinful nature.

The good news is that God has already won the victory and has given us everything we need to fight daily. If you're like me, you want to be consistent in all you do. So let's find a way to be consistent in our sports and our walk with God. Whether it's mid-season or spring break, the Devil is not relaxing, so we can't either.

WHITE BOARD CHALLENGE

Create a plan of attack. Identify when you're most likely to get off track and decide a couple ways to keep yourself focused during the vulnerable times.

FAIL BUT DON'T FEAR

When they came to the crowd, a man approached
Jesus and knelt before him. "Lord, have mercy on my
son," he said. "He has seizures and is suffering greatly.
He often falls into the fire or into the water. I brought
him to your disciples, but they could not heal him."

"You unbelieving and perverse generation," Jesus
replied, "How long shall I stay with you? How long shall
I put up with you? Bring the boy here to me." Jesus
rebuked the demon, and it came out of the boy, and he
was healed at that moment. Then the disciples came
to Jesus in private and asked, "Why couldn't we drive it
out?" He replied, "Because you have so little faith. Truly
I tell you, if you have faith as small as a mustard seed,
you can say to this mountain, 'Move from here to there,'
and it will move. Nothing will be impossible for you."

—Matthew 17:14-20 NIV

I played seven years in the NFL. What could I know
about failure?

Failure is fair, insomuch as it doesn't discriminate. It will be happy to introduce itself to everyone! The way I see it, the only way someone avoids ever failing is if they never try. If you never shoot, you will never miss. But you'll never score either.

I was cut from every NFL team I ever played for. That's right, four times I was fired. Sent packing. Given my walking papers. "Don't let the door hit you on your way out." You get the point. Failure happens to us all.

If you don't fail often, your goals are too small.

The Bible is full of examples of people dealing with failure. The disciples, for example, try to heal a boy who was possessed but they couldn't do it! Moses never made it to the Promised Land. Adam and Eve failed to obey the rules of the Garden of Eden.

We will all face failure. As athletes, we risk it every time we compete. The Bible is clear that we don't have to fear failure, because God is with us. We already know that we are supposed to run to win and that God is honored when we do our best. So let's face failure head on.

I think the bigger question is what we do once we have failed. Did the disciples ever try to heal again? Does failure shut us down and make us quit, or does it strengthen our conviction? Did we learn anything from failing?

If I had quit after the first time I got cut, I would have missed out on lots of great things. If I moved forward in fear of failure, I would have been timid and hesitant, worried more about failing than playing good football. Operating that way will never result in the best outcome.

God gives us a blueprint for living without fear. We're to trust that the Lord is always with us and is stronger than anything we might face! Failure will come, but that's just part of being imperfect humans. I'd tell you to avoid failure by being like Jesus, but I have a feeling we'll fail in that attempt.

WHITE BOARD CHALLENGE

Are you afraid of failure, or is a past failure holding you back? Face your fear today. Accept that failure is possible but that God is with you. Name three reasons to press forward. Stand up and say them out loud!

WEEK 5
DAY FOUR

GOD'S GATORADE

They will run and not grow weary; They will walk and
not grow faint.

—Isaiah 40:31 NIV

This may offend some of you, but I'm gonna go for it.
One qualification for being a respectable athlete is that
your "sport" requires a little bit of physical effort. It's
debatable, but billiards players, you're out! Bowlers can
argue they go ten frames but c'mon. At least golfers walk
miles over eighteen holes. You get my point. If I haven't
offended you and your "sport," let's continue.

When I think of athletes, I think of blood, sweat,
and tears. I know I'm the crazy one who chose football,
but still. Fatigue is almost always part of sport. Often
games become battles of attrition, and the team in
better physical condition prevails. You rugby and soccer
athletes seem to go forever!

I trained with the mindset of being in such good shape that I wouldn't get tired during the game. It didn't always work, but that was the idea.

What if there were a way for an athlete to never get tired? I never went to seminary, but it seems like that is what the prophet Isaiah is saying. "Those who hope in the Lord will run and not grow weary." Man, that would be great. I would be invincible on the field! But after a deeper look, I think Isaiah is telling us that God will be our strength. That our human body will fail, but He will be there to keep us going. That no matter how tough life gets or how hopeless it appears, we have an endless supply of power from God's Holy Spirit.

You're probably thinking, "You got all that from that one verse?" Well that verse plus the rest of the Bible. The book is pretty adamant that God loves us and will always be with us.

So when we get tired, on the field or in life— mentally, physically, or spiritually—let's remember to look to God to fill our energy bar and get us where we need to go. If that doesn't work, there's always Gatorade.

WHITE BOARD CHALLENGE

Your challenge is to encourage someone who needs it; remind them that God will sustain them in their time of need. And you'll be there too!

WEEK 5
DAY FIVE

LIFE IS TOUGH; GOD IS FAITHFUL

Has God forgotten to be gracious? Has he slammed
the door on his compassion? And I said, "This is my
fate; the Most High has turned his hand against me."
But then I recall all you have done, O Lord;
I remember your wonderful deeds of long ago.
They are constantly in my thoughts. I cannot stop
thinking about your mighty works.

—Psalm 77:9-12 NLT

I'm thirty-four years old. Old to some, not so to others.

Believe it or not, I'm writing this devotional with
my eyes. I'm using a device called an eye gaze, which is
attached to a tablet, and this allows me to control the tablet
with my eyes. Now why would I do that, other than that
it's super cool technology? Well, because I have very little
control over my hands and arms because of the disease I'm
fighting. Over the last five years my muscles have grown
weaker and weaker, and I need more and more help. I

need help with just about everything. Yup, five years ago I was smashing NFL ball carriers as a Tennessee Titan, and today I can barely use my arms. It sucks.

Do you ever get angry with God? I do. David did, as we see from Psalm 77. Have you ever been through such tough circumstances that you believe God is nowhere to be found? I have. David has.

Psalm 77 is so beautiful to me because it is so real. David, who God famously called a man after His own heart, is going through some tough times. He's on the run from people trying to kill him, and things aren't good. I believe he shows us how to be real with God. Where are you, God? Have you forgotten me? I think we've all been here, or we could be soon. David teaches us that God can handle the truth of what we're feeling. So keep it real with God.

Once we have gotten all of our grievances out, we might continue to follow David's example by remembering all the times God has been there for us, "But then I recall all you have done."

Yes, what I'm going through is incredibly difficult, but that doesn't negate all that God has done and is doing for me. He gifted me with the ability to play professional football. He has protected me from countless disasters where, by my own ignorance, I should have died. He has blessed me with unbelievable support and a purpose for living each day. He's allowing me to write this with my eyes! Yeah, life is tough, but God is faithful.

I want to be like David, so I choose to remember all that God has done.

WHITE BOARD CHALLENGE

Have an honesty session with God. Tell Him how you really feel. Maybe even say some things you've never admitted before. Be all the way real. Then remember all the good things He has done for you.

WEEK SIX:

GAME DAY

WEEK 6
DAY ONE

Whatever you do, work at it with all your heart, as
working for the Lord, not for human masters.

—Colossians 3:23 NIV

This verse smacked me upside the head when I was in
college. I mean, I had always been a workhorse, one of
the hardest working people I knew, especially when it
came to football. Pushing myself to torturous lengths.
Coming early. Staying late. Doing extra. I thrived on
outworking my opponents and teammates. The more I
worked the better I felt about myself. The more value I
thought I had.

I knew how to work for myself and to please and
impress others. But working for God? What does that
even mean, let alone look like?

Tim McGill was the campus pastor for Athletes
in Action at Penn State. He told me that verse meant I
should be working and playing my sport for an audience

of One: No, I'm not talking about your momma in the stands. I'm talking about God. He said God is pleased when you use your gifts to the best of your ability "with all your heart." And our value doesn't depend on how hard we work. Tim explained that performing for God is reflected in attitude and action. Not only will we be giving our best effort, but we'll also have a great attitude, because we already know that God approves of us. We don't need to worry about approval or acceptance, so we can just go all out and enjoy doing it!

The praise of man is fleeting. It's flaky at best. They will love you when you're on the way up and boo you the first chance they get.

But God's love is steady and reliable. Not based on my performance. He just wants my best. My whole heart. Win, lose, or draw.

To hammer this lesson home I started writing "A1" on my wrist tape on game day. When 100,000 fans were screaming in the stadium, and I was tempted to perform for the crowd, I would look at my wrist and remember: I was only playing for an audience of one.

WHITE BOARD CHALLENGE

Write down the top three reasons you work hard. If pleasing God isn't number one, ask yourself why not. Choose one way to help you remember that you're supposed to be working to please God. Is it a picture in your locker, a phrase you repeat, or something else cool?

WEEK 6
DAY TWO

Be sober-minded; be watchful. Your adversary the devil prowls around like a roaring lion, seeking someone to devour. Resist him, firm in your faith, knowing that the same kinds of suffering are being experienced by your brotherhood throughout the world.

—1 Peter 5: 8-9 ESV

Have you ever noticed that teams don't game plan for the players who ride the bench? Coaches don't worry about players who have little or no impact on the game!

Every team that wants to win, almost without exception, has a game plan. Granted, some are more detailed and meticulous than others, but the old adage holds true, "Failing to plan is planning to fail." In team sports, the opposition's best players must be accounted for. Typically, the best players are the reason for the game plan in the first place.

I always wanted to be on the opponent's scouting report. I wanted them to have to worry about me! I knew that if I was doing a good enough job then they would have to account for me on game day and, probably, all week leading up to the game. I knew that if I was getting double teamed when I ran down on kickoff, that they respected the way I played. I took it as a compliment.

This really is the way that our spiritual lives play out too. First, we must be aware that there is a battle going on all around us. The Bible says that the Devil prowls the earth like a lion looking to steal, kill, and destroy. This is serious business! I told my friend last week not to be surprised when she is attacked, because if she is a prayer warrior for the good guys, then she should expect a battle. The enemy is going after the one shooting at them, not the one sleeping. Once we're aware of the battle, we need to get involved. Get out there and be a force!

Listen, is the opponent game planning for you? Are you on the Devil's scouting report as someone to account for? Or are you on the bench? It's safer there. If you don't step out and rock the boat maybe no one will notice what you say you believe. If you keep quiet when there is wrong happening around you, then they can't look at you differently. But that's not really living. Nor is it believing, because belief is proven in action.

So get in the game! Make an impact! Make the opponent put you on their dangerous list. It won't be easy, but if you want easy you're probably playing the wrong game. God will be with you every step. So get your game face on, and let's go!

WHITE BOARD CHALLENGE

Choose an area where you can get more involved in the battle for God's Kingdom and take the first step in moving towards it. Maybe there's an organization you can help, or someone you need to talk to, or another action you have been avoiding. Make that move and show the opponent you're a force to be reckoned with!

WEEK 6
DAY THREE

Now the Lord is the Spirit, and where the Spirit of the
Lord is, there is freedom.

—2 Corinthians 3:17 ESV

Have you ever gotten to a place in the game
where you felt free? You aren't worried about the coach
reprimanding you or the fans booing. You're free to
move and decide and flow inside the confines of the
game. You may make mistakes, but you're free to do so.
All your training and practice is taking over. You're not
untouchable, but the game is easy in a way that removes
all pressure.

Most athletes don't reach this place. We're too
bogged down by pressure from internal and external
forces: parents, coaches, teammates, critics, and
ourselves. We don't allow ourselves to experience the
freedom of enjoying the game.

As Paul writes to the church in Galatia, "It is for freedom that Christ has set us free" (Galatians 5:1 NIV). God offers us freedom, too. Yes, freedom from death but also freedom to live. A lot of us are held down by rules and regulations. We see God as this giant authority looking down from above waiting for us to mess up so He can strike us down. But that's not who He is. Belief in God means freedom in His love. Like our sports, there are rules to play by. These are for the fairness and safety of ourselves and others. Within those rules, we are free to run and play and decide. We don't need to worry about the coach berating us or the crowds shaming us with boos. We are free to do our best and enjoy it.

It won't all be scoring and winning; there will be losing, too. There will be hard times and struggles as well. But the freedom is in knowing that God will be with you through it all.

I know this message is tough for some of you to agree with or understand. You've never felt free a day in your life. Some of you feel enslaved to abuse or addiction, or the approval of others. But I want you to know that you don't have to feel that way forever. There is freedom available for all of us. If you've been stuck for a while, seek help. There are plenty of people trained to help you find freedom from whatever is enslaving you.

For some of us, we use our sport as our getaway from real life. But I believe that if we can find freedom in our sport, then there's hope for real life, too.

WHITE BOARD CHALLENGE

See if you can experience freedom today. When you train, practice, or play, have a mindset of freedom. Concentrate on God's gifts of athleticism. Do your best to ignore all else.

HOLY TRASH TALK!

Do not let any unwholesome talk come out of your mouths, but only what is helpful for building others up according to their needs, that it may benefit those who listen.

—Ephesians 4:29 NIV

Boy-oh-boy, do we athletes know how to talk trash! It's part of our culture. We joke around with each other in the locker room, call each other out on the practice field, and defend each other on game day while we verbally attack anything wearing the opposite colored uniform.

I have to believe that the NFL has some of the best trash talk among all sports. With those helmets on, guys will say just about anything. I've heard some reckless, dirty, mean stuff on the field. So how do we stay Christ-like with that going on? Do we have to fit in, or can we rise above the garbage chatter?

I'm a firm believer in letting my game do the talking. Who cares what they say if I'm whipping them? But I know some people have to talk. So just remember that you represent Christ. It limits your vocabulary and forces you to be creative. But you can still have fun and get your point across. Yes, to be clear, I believe it's possible to talk "trash" while honoring God!

Another tactic is to turn it into love. You might not believe the look you get when you volley an opponent's cursing tirade with "God loves you." Ha! I know it's corny, but it will mess with their minds and give you the mental advantage. The way I see it, if you're mentally strong enough to control your emotions to say something not vulgar or hurtful, then you've got them whooped anyway.

God made us to compete ferociously and give our best, but we are also called to control our tongue. Play the game so loud that everyone can't help but notice how quiet you were.

WHITE BOARD CHALLENGE

Go out and talk some holy trash today! Whether it's a friendly game of ping pong or your dual meet, have fun representing God with your speech as you compete hard.

LIGHT UP THE FIELD

In the same way, let your light shine before others,
that they may see your good deeds and glorify
your Father in heaven.

—Matthew 5:16 NIV

Every Saturday in the fall, more than 100,000 fans pour into Beaver Stadium to root on the Penn State football team. I can't explain the way the adrenaline pumps through your body when you run onto the field and all 100,000 erupt. I still shake my head in disbelief thinking how God allowed me to influence people on that platform.

Whatever we're doing and whoever is watching, we're called to bring glory to God by the good things we do. Yes, that includes playing your sport. Pretty cool. The way you play the game, regardless of talent level, you can bring glory to God. You never know how performing with integrity, passion, and conviction could influence your opponent, a teammate, or someone watching from the stands.

Today's verse talks about letting "your light shine." Well the thing about light is that it's meant for everyone. The only way to avoid light is to cover your eyes or to hide. Or the one shining the light can put it out. Your "light" is your life. You are the light! And right now being an athlete is part of your life. Don't hide your light or stop it from shining. Take every workout, practice, and competition as an opportunity to share your light with the world around you. This includes far more than your physical performance. Everything you do can be a witness. How you treat the officials and the other team. How you react to a bad call. How you handle winning and losing. Your light can shine through all of it.

What you say matters too, before, during, and after the game. Remember where you got your abilities, and always try to point people to God.

What an honor to play for God's glory. If there are 100,000 or 10 watching, let's point all eyes to God above.

WHITE BOARD CHALLENGE

I love when an athlete does something good and then silently points to the heavens. Of course I don't know the athlete's motives, but I see that as acknowledging God. A small gesture to say, "Don't look at me, look at God." Take time today to thank God for your athletic ability and the fact that you get to play sports! Commit that you will play to point people to God rather than yourself.

IDENTITY

IT'S WHO YOU ARE

Yet to all who did receive him, to those who believed in his name, he gave the right to become children of God.

—John 1:12 NIV

Football was pretty much everything to me. I would have said that faith and family came first, but my actions said otherwise. For about sixteen years of my life, football was the center of my universe. I set my schedule by it. It dictated what I ate, when I slept, where I traveled. It was in about ninety-eight percent of my conversations. Heck, I even dreamed about it. By all rational accounts, my identity was wrapped up in the game.

Looking back on it, I was one of the lucky ones. I had people telling me that I was more than a ball player. I had a college degree and should have been able to get a different job when I finished playing. I had faith in God and at least knew in my head that God didn't value me because I was an athlete. Most of the athletes I knew didn't have the set of cards I carried. And I was still caught up thinking football was first and foremost!

The problem with having our identity in anything other than being a child of God is that everything else is temporary and unreliable. We know that our bodies can't perform like we want them to forever. Even with modern medicine and technology, there is still a limit. Whether you retire after high school or your tenth Olympics, one day you'll be an ex-athlete. If your sport is who you are, then who are you when you can no longer participate? If you find your value from your sport, when it's over, do you still feel valued? If your sport is the most important thing, when it's gone, what is left for you to care for?

God says that not only are we His children, but that we are His prized possession. He cares about all that we do, and we can call on Him day or night. God will never leave us or give up on us. We can always count on Him. He promises to guide us along the way. His character is never changing and His love is never ending. In other words, we should have our identity in

Christ. He is the one truly reliable thing in this world. So when you lose your job or get bad news from the doctor, your identity, Christ, is rock solid. When the coach benches you or your body can't perform like you want, you may be shaken, but your foundation is sturdy.

Christ doesn't claim to smooth life over or remove any difficulty, but He does promise to go through everything with you. I can't think of a better anchor to attach my identity to than the unchanging love of God.

WHITE BOARD CHALLENGE

Name three things that compete to be your identity. Sports? Grades? Money? Job? Good, now you can put them in the right spot, under your relationship with God.

YOU SEE SHEEP HERDER, GOD SEES KING

David ran and stood over him. He took hold of the
Philistine's sword and drew it from the sheath.
After he killed him, he cut off his head with the sword.
When the Philistines saw that their hero was dead,
they turned and ran.

—1 Samuel 17:51 NIV

There's no way after reading verse 51 that anyone could think that David wasn't a beast of a warrior. There's no way he couldn't have been Samuel's first pick for king. But going back to Chapter 16, we see that all seven of David's brothers were brought to Samuel as likely candidates for king before David. That's when God dropped one of the all-time classic wisdom bombs!

"But the LORD said to Samuel, 'Do not consider his appearance or his height, for I have rejected him [the oldest brother]. The LORD does not look at the things people look at. People look at the outward appearance, but the LORD looks at the heart'" (1 Samuel 16: 7 NIV).

After all seven brothers were rejected, David, the smallest and youngest, was called in from the field where he was tending sheep, and he was anointed king.

I have to say, this is one I can't relate to. I was always pretty much the biggest. Definitely never the smallest. And rarely, if ever, was I overlooked. I'm going to spare you my sob story about having 163 players selected ahead of me in the NFL Draft. I don't want you weeping.

This is the world of sports, in a big way. Athletes are judged on physical appearance first and then athletic ability. In a lot of cases, character comes later. The heart of a player matters, but only if they keep you around long enough to see it. So this is how we are conditioned to operate. Value people by what they bring to the table, their potential for contribution.

What if God valued us that way? Half of you just thought "I'd be fine." Well, y'all need to read my fantastic book called *Humility: the Best Thing about Me*. You're the half who, like me, are taller or stronger and think it's not our fault we're at the top of the gene pool. The other half thought, "Well, that would suck. God was the only one who doesn't discriminate against me, because I'm vertically challenged." If God worked that way, then it really would be survival of the fittest. But just like the story of David, the Bible is plum full of examples of people doing amazing work for God, people who aren't first team all-conference, and some probably even struggled to make the team.

What about those of us who have struggled with judging books by their covers? For me, I have learned that I need God's grace even more.

You're probably either used to being judged all the time, or you're used to being the judge. I admit, I'm the judge more often than not. This is the way of the world, but not God's way. We are all equally valuable in His sight. We can all take a lesson from Samuel and David. Stop judging people by what they look like and stop worrying about what people think. The fruits of the Spirit are clear, and they shine through God's people. So just show up and let the fruit of the Spirit put you right where you need to be. It may be at the top of the batting order or the team statistician, but either way, give God the glory.

WHITE BOARD CHALLENGE

Honesty time. Are you the judge or the judged? Where do you find yourself valuing people differently than you should? Next time you catch yourself in the act of putting people in value order, drop down and do a pushup to remind yourself that God loves all equally. That's right, one pushup wherever you are. I dare you.

WEEK 7
DAY THREE

BE LIKE BARRY

Humble yourselves before the Lord,
and he will lift you up.

—James 4:10 NIV

When I played, I knew I was the best. At least that's what I convinced myself. I've always believed that to play at the highest level, you have to believe in yourself more than anyone else does. "If I don't love me, who will?" I used to say. This was my mental advantage. Someone might be more talented or gifted than me, but I would find a way to win.

From a pure competition perspective, I still believe this. And I actually believe that you can be humble while thinking this way. Believing you're a great player doesn't mean you have to be conceited or a bad teammate. See, while I believed in my abilities and believed that I wouldn't be beaten, I didn't believe that I was more important than anybody else. And that's really the definition of humility, "a modest or low view of one's own importance."

The best players don't have to tell anybody they're the best or act superior to others in order to elevate themselves. Anyone watching who knows anything about the sport can typically tell who the better players are. It usually isn't the loudest bragging mouth anyway. God has promised that if we're humble, He will lift us up. Best player or not, the humble person will be honored.

It's tough to see the humble being honored in today's world with ESPN and social media. Seems like the more we promote ourselves, the more fortune and fame we get. The more outwardly confident we are, the more attention we get. God doesn't promise fortune and fame but that we will be honored as He would honor us. I don't know exactly what God's honor looks like, but I have to believe that it's better than fifteen minutes of fame or a pocket full of cash.

That's one of the reasons I admire Barry Sanders. Even as one of the greatest running backs in NFL history, when Barry scored a touchdown, he simply handed the ball to the official and celebrated with his teammates. He would make defenders look silly as they tried to tackle him, but he never taunted them or showboated. He simply went about his business like a true pro, on his way to the Hall of Fame. He knew he was at the top of his sport, on the biggest stage, but he didn't need to brag or belittle anyone else.

If Sanders can be humble at the highest level, then I know I too can be humble right here. Sure, he had confidence through the roof, but he also had an inner attitude of humility that was reflected in his actions. God has called us to play with humility. Do you believe in yourself? Do you perform with confidence? Are you after God's honor or man's praise?

WHITE BOARD CHALLENGE

Be humble today. Choose a specific action to show humility. Maybe it's doing a job assigned to freshmen, or being last in the food line. Find a way to be humble. Oh, and you can't tell anybody you're doing it. That's the whole point.

CAN A LION LOVE A BUCKEYE?

[The lawyer] answered, "'Love the Lord your God with all your heart and with all your soul and with all your strength and with all your mind' and, 'Love your neighbor as yourself.'" "You have answered correctly," Jesus replied. "Do this and you will live."

—Luke 10:27-28 NIV

You know what word you don't hear a lot during a game? Love. In football, like a lot of sports, there's so much aggression and physicality, the last thing that seems to belong is love. Does love belong in sports? Or do we just go back to that loving feeling after we smash each other on the field? The Bible talks a lot about love, including instructing us to love our neighbor.

Okay, I'll love my teammates.

No, not good enough. The Bible clearly shows us that we should love our neighbor, and often that's the last person in the world that we want to love. I'm talking about myself, a Penn State Nittany Lion. And I'm supposed to love a Buckeye from Ohio State? That's hard to even write. But that's what God wants from us. We're to love all people regardless of race, status, or ethnicity. Yes, even the scarlet and gray-clad players of Ohio State (or as they like to say, "The Ohio State").

So is there room for love in sports? Yeah there's always room for love. That definitely doesn't mean you play with any less physicality, but it does mean that you care about your opponent as a human being and treat them with respect. You don't have to help them off the ground and hug them, but you certainly can't spit on them and throw cheap shots.

Love looks different between the playing lines. It looks like fierce, clean competition—and a handshake when the dust settles.

It comes down to this: Honor God with how you play. And where God is, there is love.

WHITE BOARD CHALLENGE

Think of your most hated rival. Relax, you don't have to go hug them or anything. Just repeat after me: They are God's children, too. So after I beat them, I will love them.

WEEK 7

DAY FIVE

WILL THIS BE ON THE TEST?

Search me, O God, and know my heart;
test me and know my anxious thoughts.
Point out anything in me that offends you,
and lead me along the path of everlasting life.

—Psalms 139:23-24 NLT

In college and the pros, we were constantly evaluated. So much so that we would get a grade after each game. I thought grades were for the academic arena! We would be graded down to the most minute details like foot placement and angle of attack. And larger items like assignments, effort, and production.

The idea is that every aspect makes a difference. From the smallest detail on up to the bigger more obvious aspects of the game. The more we can do correctly, the better we played, the better our team would be, the more we could win.

Asking God to point out our shortcomings is like asking for a game day grade. Seems pretty risky, I know. Trust me. We dreaded that grade sheet sometimes. Even more so we dreaded being called out in front of the team while we watched the game film. But we knew it was for our own good and the good of the team. Most of us cringe at the thought of having our faults and shortcomings highlighted for us. Yet again, it's for our own benefit.

God isn't up above with a grade sheet waiting to point out all our wrongs, but He does love when we ask Him to show us where we are messing up, because it grows our relationship with Him and expands our self-awareness.

Unlike my coaches, God doesn't keep a record of our mistakes. Once we receive the correction, He marks our score as "forgiven" and then moves on, always wanting the best for us.

After we reviewed the film, received the grade and coaching points, it was up to us to learn from our mistakes and improve. You better believe our coaches hated when we made the same mistakes twice. I'm sure

God doesn't like it either, but at least we know He'll forgive us. That's more than I can say about some coaches I've had.

Let's ask God to search our hearts, knowing that in His love He will show us what's best.

WHITE BOARD CHALLENGE

During your quiet time today, spend some time asking God to open your eyes to anything in your life you've become blind to. Then sit and listen for a while.

WEEK EIGHT:

GOOD RUN

WEEK 8
DAY ONE

So those who are last now will be first then, and those who are first will be last . . . For even the Son of Man came not to be served but to serve others and to give his life as a ransom for many.

—Matthew 20:16, 28 NLT

I played for Jacksonville for a short nine months. Five games to end a season, the full off-season, and four preseason games. Though short, that time was very impactful for me. During the final week of the season I was there, I approached the team Chaplain and said, "Hey, if you hear of any service opportunities, I'm interested. I feel like I need more in my life." He immediately told me about a trip to Costa Rica scheduled for that off-season. If I went, he would consider going too.

That March we went to San José, Costa Rica, along with another teammate and a couple other NFL guys. Our main task was to build a fence around a compound that became a site for a school and some housing for mothers and children. We had an amazing time and did some good work along the way. I felt something as I worked. Corny as it may sound, it was as if all was right in the world. I was doing what I was meant to do.

The service bug had infiltrated our team. Led by AJ, our Chaplain, we built a culture of service amongst the Jaguars. We did work projects, helped at soup kitchens, spoke to youth programs, visited kids in hospitals, and more. That off-season was so fun and fulfilling because we had a group of guys who were inspired to serve.

In case you don't know yet, we were made to serve. Jesus lived the ultimate example as His life was defined by doing for others with love. He consistently showed us how to put the needs of others ahead of our own. That's really what service is: doing for someone what you don't have to do because you can. As athletes, we are so blessed with ability. Ability to work, talk, give, love. There are a million and one ways to serve. You can go across the world or down the hall to your sister's room. It could take a second (like picking up a piece of trash or opening a door for someone), a couple of hours (like mentoring at the local boys and girls club), or years and years (like moving to Haiti to help rebuild a community).

Service is an attitude. If your heart is open to it, and your eyes are looking for it, there's opportunity to serve everywhere. Be intentional. Seek out ways to use your unique talents and interests to fill a need for someone else. You won't be sorry. Service is one of those things where the more you give, it seems the more you get back in return.

Since Jacksonville, I've served all over the world in all types of ways. I'm not trying to pat myself on the back, believe me, I do enough of that. I say this to make the point that without service, I feel like something is missing in my life. I am as convinced of this as I am of anything in this life: we are built to serve!

WHITE BOARD CHALLENGE

Serve. Today, I challenge you to commit two small acts of service. And if you really wanna push yourself, find an opportunity to serve on a regular basis. Now watch God work through you.

ON TURF AS IT IS IN HEAVEN

In this manner, therefore, pray: Our Father in heaven, hallowed be Your name. Your kingdom come. Your will be done on earth as it is in heaven. Give us this day our daily bread. And forgive us our debts, as we forgive our debtors.. And do not lead us into temptation, but deliver us from the evil one. For Yours is the kingdom and the power and the glory forever. Amen.

—Matthew 6:9-13 NKJV

As far back as I can remember, before every football game, the team would take a knee, bow their heads, join hands, and recite the Lord's Prayer. Then we would get up, get crazy, and go rip someone's head off. I mean from Pop Warner to the Tennessee Titans and every stop in between, we prayed. Actually, most teams I've been around would recite this prayer before and after the game!

I never thought this to be odd until I got older and realized that not everyone believed in God like I did.

But there's just something about God and sports that go together. No matter what we believed individually, we all prayed this prayer together. It's just what we did. What everyone who plays the game did, as far as I could tell. Call it tradition, call it ritual, call it superstition. Athletes will do just about anything if we think it will help our game.

In college, a group of us started saying a quick prayer after practice and inviting our teammates to join. My friend Nick had the idea to go through the Lord's Prayer and explain it a little bit each day. I mean, we're all praying it on Saturdays. Maybe we should understand it!

So Nick went through the prayer piece by piece, and it was awesome. He explained that this was Jesus teaching us how to pray. The prayer is a template for talking to God. It's God showing us that He wants to bring heaven down to our turf. Most of the guys, including me, had never really understood the meaning before.

You can imagine how meaningful it became when we knelt together before a game. Now we actually understood what we were praying, and with an extra sense of God with us, we'd go out and try to rip someone's head off.

WHITE BOARD CHALLENGE

Read the Lord's Prayer and keep in mind some of these key points: Acknowledge to God that He is holy and awesome—the King of the Universe. We seek to do His will now, on the turf that God's put in front of us today (perhaps best summed up with "love others"). God will give us what we need for today. We've been forgiven, big time, so we too need to forgive people we think have wronged us. God will steer us clear from bad situations and protect us from the Devil's schemes. God is worthy of our praise and worship. Now, if you want to get crazy, invite someone to join you in reading this prayer.

THE GIFT

The world and its desires pass away, but whoever does
the will of God lives forever.

—1 John 2:17 NIV

At thirty years old, I retired from being a professional
athlete. That didn't mean my life and love of sports
were over, just that I wouldn't play as a job anymore.
A month after retiring, I was diagnosed with ALS. And
that would prove to number my days being able to play
sports at all. You better believe I played golf until it was
more hassle than it was enjoyable. The last time I golfed,
I had one friend stabilizing me and another helping me
grip the club and address the ball.

I tell you all of this to say, hold loosely the things
of this world. They will pass.

Our bodies age and our reflexes slow. Yeah, we all
know that our time as athletes will give way to becoming

former athletes. But I urge you to view your ability to play as a gift from God with an expiration date. Getting to play one season is fun, and God let me keep that gift for almost nineteen years! I'm spoiled. We don't know when the gift may expire; that's one reason we should make the most of it while we have it. If we view being an athlete as a right or something we deserve, then when we become former athletes we will be angry, bitter, or jaded.

God is very clear. We are first and foremost to love Him. That doesn't mean we can't love all that life has to offer. After all, Jesus came that we "may have life and have it abundantly" (John 10:10 ESV). We just need to have things in their place of importance, behind God. If we are hanging tightly to anything other than God, one day, sooner or later, we will lose it.

After retiring from football, I was a little angry. Angry at the game (I was sure I could still play), at the NFL (it just wasn't fair), and at the current players (I know I'm better than THAT guy!). I made sure to schedule my tee times for midday on Sundays, so to miss most of the NFL games. I felt the game did me wrong somehow or owed me something.

It was over. I needed to let it go.

Through counseling, time, and lots of prayer, I came to realize what a gift football had been to me. And that the gift had an expiration date. And I was fortunate to have had the gift for so long, to have had the gift at all.

But God brought the game back to me or, rather, me to it. Three seasons detached from the game, the Titans hired Mike Mularkey as head coach, and he invited me to speak to the team. Through a series of events, I became involved with the team on a weekly basis and was given the honor and notation of "Titan for Life."

See, whatever it is that you are valuing more than you should, God's just waiting for you to loosen your grip so there's room to gift you with something else, something better.

I'll never play football again, but I'm gonna enjoy the gift of being involved with sports again. That is, until the expiration date comes up.

WHITE BOARD CHALLENGE

Write down what your gift is. Playing a sport? Running fast? Maybe you have multiple gifts.

Now write how long you would keep the gift were it up to you. Then write in big bold letters right on top of the length of time you just wrote, "ONLY GOD!"

BEST OVER GOOD

"I have the right to do anything," you say—but not everything is beneficial. "I have the right to do anything"—but not everything is constructive.

—1 Corinthians 10:23 NIV

Man, I loved the dining hall in college. We called it training table at Penn State, but it's just the place where the football team ate its meals. Of course, it was all you can eat, and some of our linemen put that to the test. They always had multiple options for us, typically a few healthy options, then a few not-so-healthy choices.

I swear, at twenty years old I could eat whatever I wanted and not give a second thought. We worked out so much that my body didn't discriminate against calories of any type.

There were some guys trying to lose weight or cut fat, and others doing anything they could to gain a pound or two. Football is funny that way. So there are all the food options a college kid could want, and it's up to us to decide what is right for us.

Today's passage is very applicable to both our lives and our sports. God has given us free will, because I'm assuming robots are boring to him. So we are faced with choices all day long. Even when our coaches demand xyz, it's still our choice to comply or not. Just like walking into training table, I still have all these options of things to do, say, and be. God is saying, "Hey, you are free to choose any of these. They aren't all good for you. Some are just okay. They won't all get you the results you really want, but you're welcome to them. Stay up late playing video games or rest well for tomorrow's workout. Go to that party that you know will be on the edge of trouble, or not." I've been there, and you better believe I've made the poor choice at times. But often, there are options that are best. This is what God wants for us. The very best. But He will always let us choose. The more we grow in relationship with God, the better we can identify the poor choice and the best option. Trust that like anything, it's a process.

This passage deserves a deeper look, of course, to fully grasp the concept of permissible versus beneficial. The way I look at it, it's tough to give instructions that can apply to everyone, so this is one of those cases in the Bible where God acknowledged that we are all different, and what is good for you may not be good for me. It's helpful to keep this in mind when I'm choking down a plate of broccoli and plain chicken, and my buddy is devouring his second serving of brownies and ice cream. We are all different, so too spiritually. I may need to be held accountable for my selection of TV shows I watch, where those same shows may be no problem for you.

This is our spiritual walk. God wants the best for us, so let's keep searching to know Him better and figure out what "best" is.

WHITE BOARD CHALLENGE

Choose best over good. Find an opportunity today to choose the best option over the good enough option. It might jump out at you, or you might have to look hard.

RUN TO WIN

Do you not know that in a race all the runners run,
but only one gets the prize? Run in such a way
as to get the prize.

—1 Corinthians 9:24 NIV

I once tried to calculate how much I've run over the span
of my athletic career. More than two decades of down
and backs, laps around the track, miles on the treadmill,
and 40-yard dashes. I lose count after eighth grade track
season, but my high school basketball teammates can
attest that we seemingly ran a marathon each week.
Needless to say, it's impossible to even guesstimate a
somewhat accurate quantity. Maybe the better question
is "how many of those runs did I run to win?" Or "how
many did I just want to make it through or not finish
last?" I played running back in high school and scored
over 130 touchdowns and rushed for 7,800 yards. At

the time, those were Michigan State records. Okay, I'll say it. That's a lot of yards! But I wasn't counting them as I was running. I didn't know much back then, but I knew that every single time I got to carry the football I wanted to score. So I ran for the end zone as if my life depended on it. I wanted to win!

God has gifted us with a life on earth and given each of us different abilities and passions to pursue. We weren't meant to wander lackadaisically through life but to passionately go after the things that matter to us. We were meant to go full speed with a purpose, attracting people to Christ by the way we live. That means that when you're doing your job, try and be the best in the business. When you're at home, be the best son or daughter you can. And when you're competing in your sport…WIN!

God actually cares how we spend our time, talents, and money. Not to compare ourselves to each other but to do our best. The longer I live the more I recognize that God cares about every aspect of my life. He wants me to thrive in relationships, at work or school and in my sport. He wants me to try and win! He's not so concerned with how many touchdowns I score, just that I run to win every time I get the ball.

WHITE BOARD CHALLENGE

Win today! Pick an activity on your calendar today and see what it's like to attack it full speed. If it's worth doing, it's worth giving a winning effort and attitude.

POST SEASON:

A FEW THOUGHTS FROM TIM

NO GREATER VICTORY

As the last few seconds ticked off the clock in Spartan stadium, I knew we had finally done it. By beating Michigan State that day, we had earned the Big Ten Champion title! It was the culmination of countless hours and sacrifices given by a hundred players and coaches to achieve a special team milestone.

I remember the hugs and celebration on the field! Every teammate, coach, and staff member involved, I think I hugged every single one of them. I don't think I stopped smiling for a month. The linebacker group got together for a picture to memorialize the victorious moment in time.

The celebration went on and on. From the field to the locker room to the plane and straight off the plane to the victory pep rally! And believe me, it didn't stop there!

Have you had a championship experience like this? This is what it should be like when we find Jesus. There really is no greater victory. The Bible tells us that the kingdom of God is like a great treasure. When we find it, we should sell everything else to keep it. Nothing else matters! What could be greater than finding the gift of salvation offered by Jesus? But in the world today we struggle to see it that way.

Regardless of how we view it, the truth is that we were all headed for eternal defeat until Jesus stepped in and took the loss, so that we can have victory forever. The championship of the universe!

WHITE BOARD CHALLENGE

If you know Jesus personally, then celebrate! Do something to celebrate the greatest victory of your life. Have some cake, throw a party! Celebrate.

ACKNOWLEDGEMENTS

Richard, without your idea and prompting, this book would have never happened. Reggie, your wisdom is always helpful. Thank you to all the people who have poured wisdom into my life over the years. I hope I'm able to pass along even a fraction of what I've been given.

TIM SHAW

Former linebacker Tim Shaw's seven years in the NFL included seasons with the Carolina Panthers, Jacksonville Jaguars, the Chicago Bears, and the Tennessee Titans. A graduate of Penn State, he also holds an MBA from George Washington University. Now an entrepreneur, Tim is a TEDx speaker and winner of the 2018 ALS Association Hero Award. Tim's first book, *Blitz Your Life*, won two Benjamin Franklin Awards in 2018 for Cover Design and the Bill Fisher Memorial Award for Best First Book by a new publisher. *On Turf as It Is in Heaven* is Tim's second book.

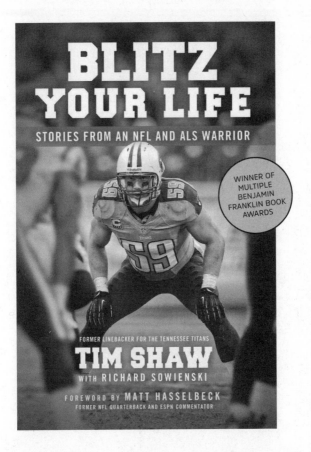